Kurt Hentschläger's immersive works SOL, ZEE and FEED begin with perceptual sensation, grounding the audience in the moment at hand. They ask for and instill a loss of control, transcend the boundaries between the observer and the observed and cannot be meaningfully documented, but must be experienced instead. The aim of this book is to look at the concepts and evoke the atmosphere of the works.

Isabelle Meiffert

DISTANZ

SPLENDID VOIDS

The Immersive Works of
Kurt Hentschläger

SOL – installation 2017
ZEE – installation 2008
FEED – performance 2005

Lights lower – blackness – fog seeps through the
collision – another body – who? – recoil sideway
another – begin to see – gray – white – yellowis
wind – flash – blindness – blackness there – gra
light – black corona – intercepted cool air curr
bing – breathing regular, irregular, regular agai
listening – stop feeling – breathe – can't – bre
bodies – too many – move left – more left – can
pulse lights – illuminate fog – feel it – softened
two – three – fog thickens – forming – forms – no
as – image – object – structure – human? – no –
humidity – anxiety rising – yellow hue – floor
regular, irregular, regular again – heartbeat – pu
breathe – can't – breathe – can – can – breathe –
normal – stroboscope – pulse lights – illuminate
kaleidoscopic hues – two – three – four-dimensi
Wall? Where is the wall? Feel with feet. The flo
the earth beneath it. Light – beam – projection –
floating in space

– I move slowly – feel the floor – extend hands –
ead – ohh – a wall – step right – another step –
gin to feel – moist – warm air thickens – sudden
emerges – turns white – afterimage – spherical
ows in – turns warm in stasis – temples throb-
artbeat – pulse – pulse – PULSE – !PULSE! – stop
can't – breathe – can – can – breathe – light –
e – normal – breath – is – normal – stroboscope –
venly dispersed – creating kaleidoscopic hues –
– forms a screen – for light – focus – taking form
ation – humanoid – fog density accumulating –
oot – steadiness temples throbbing – breathing
ulse – PULSE – !PULSE! – stop – breathe – can't –
– bodies – can breathe – normal – breath – is –
eel it – softened and evenly dispersed – creating
ructures in constant animation – Nothing solid.
till have the floor. And the earth. There must be
– colliding – floating – mid air – somersaulting –

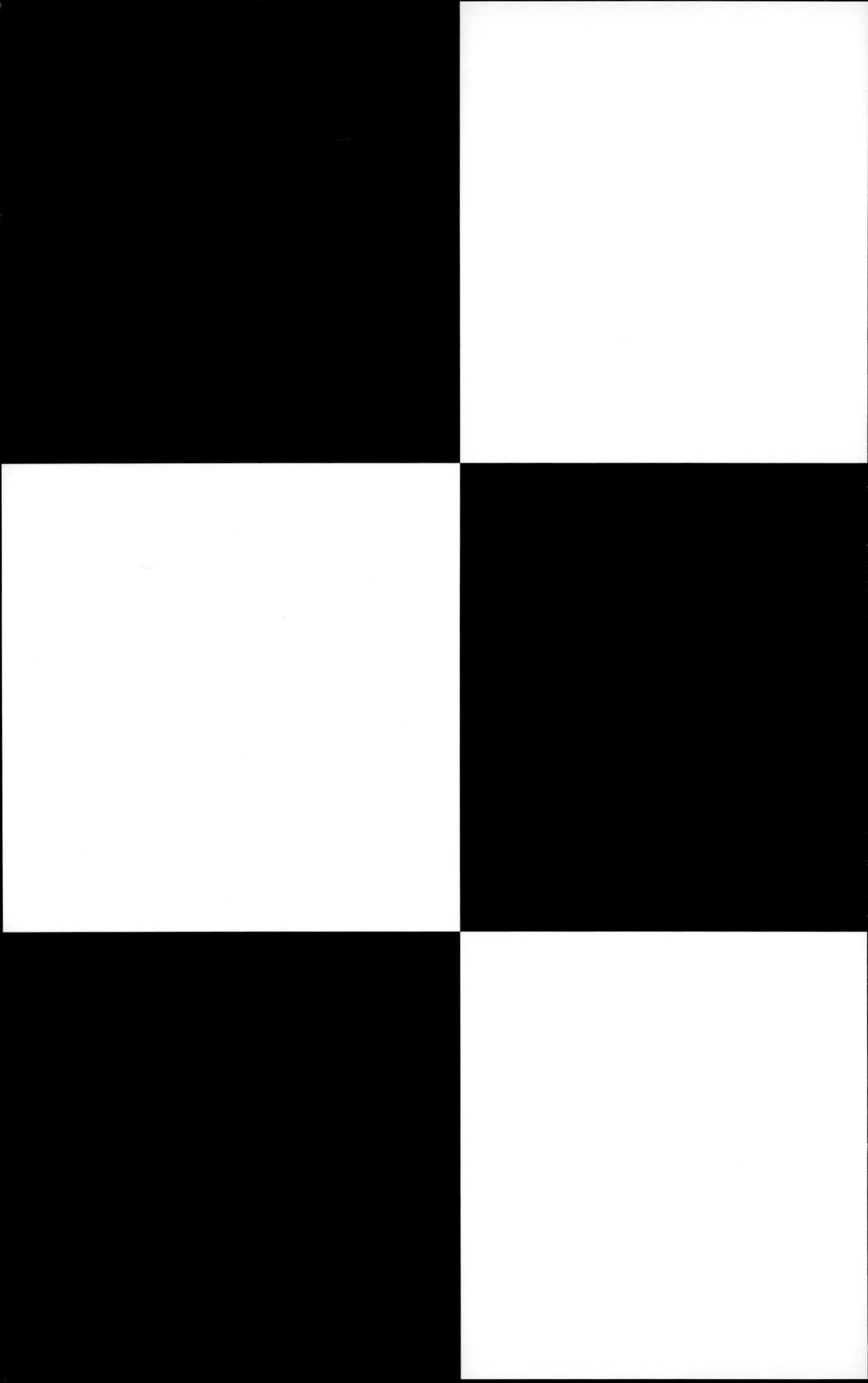

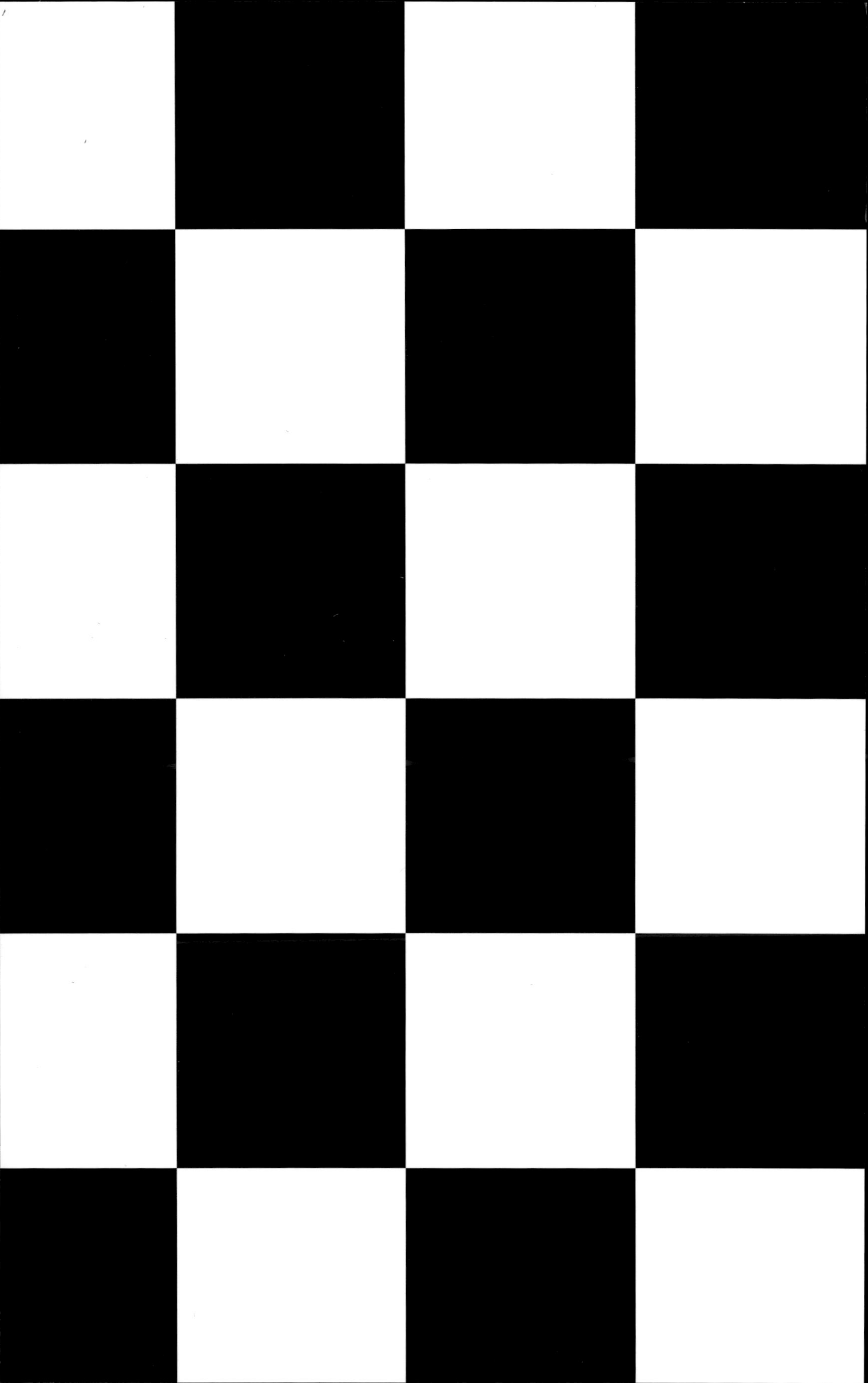

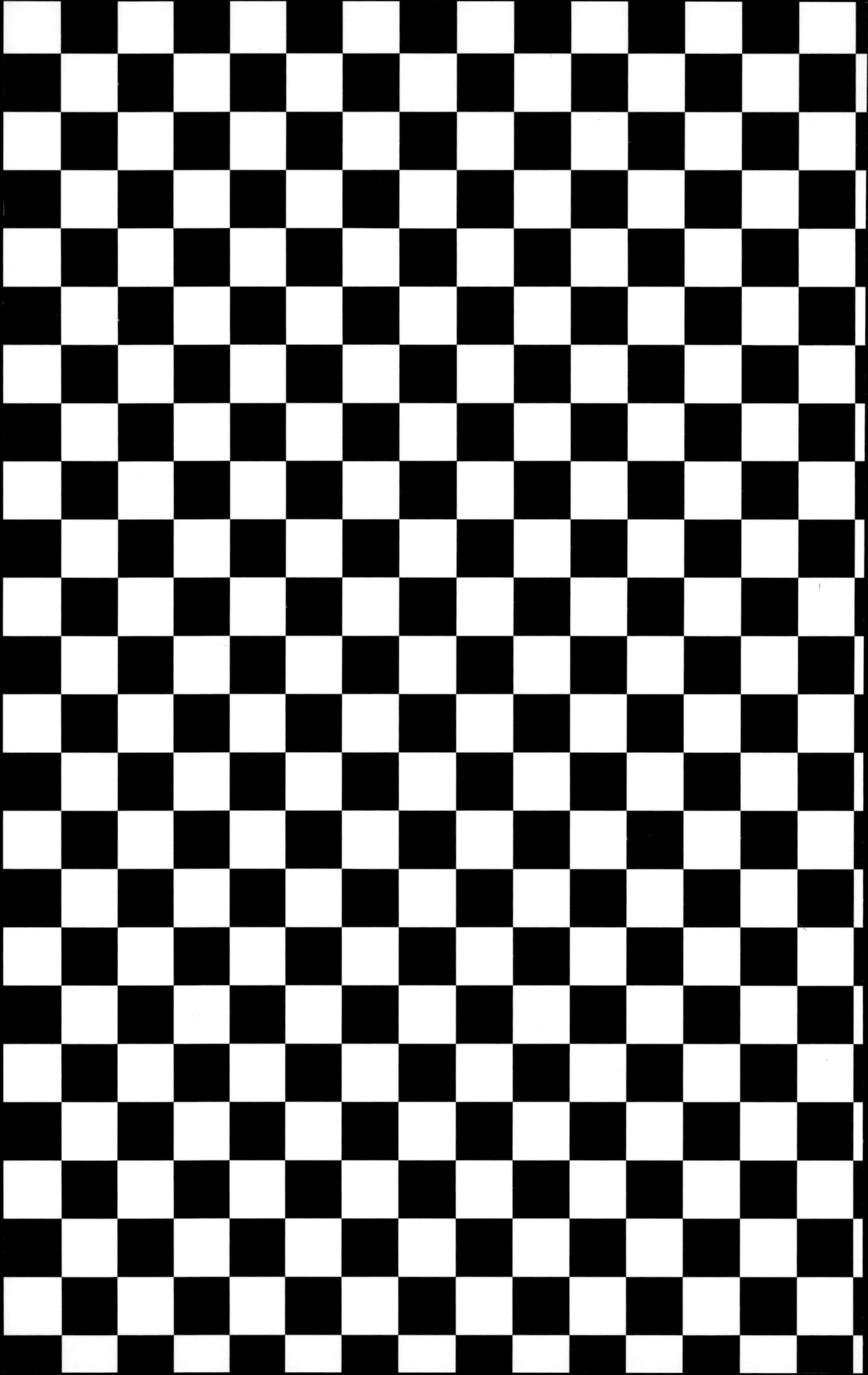

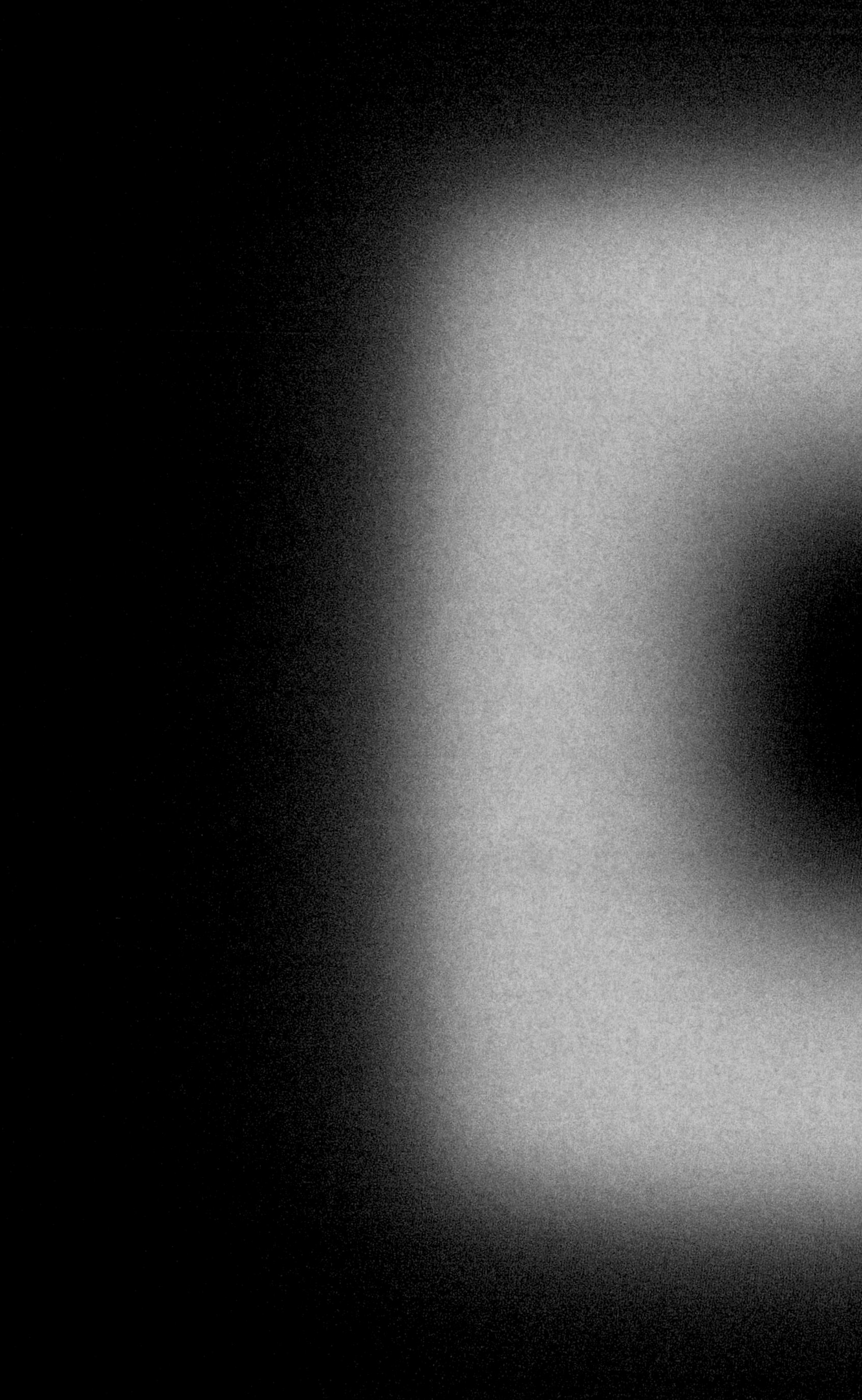

The Splendid Phenomenology of Hentschlägerian Voids

G. Roger Denson

Kurt Hentschläger's insight into performance and screenings is intentionally oppositional to logic, method and generalization, all of which intrude on our experience of phenomena. Logic, method and generalization block our reception of spatial and experiential stimulation. They artificially direct thought to the assumed *common features* of experience rather than acknowledge and enhance the singularity and spontaneity of an individual's experience-in-the-moment. Even the words used here to describe and analyze the work are an infringement on the splendid phenomenology of Hentschlägerian voids; what the artist calls his installational, interperformative, intersubjective attempts to share experience with others. But what experiences should be shared? Phenomena? There can be nothing else; but *as* what? Hentschläger has settled on calling it phenomenology; the experience of consciousness, experiencing without imposing boundaries that distinguish the experience from the consciousness of experience. Yet why distinguish what is not distinguishable? Is it because experience must be of something, just as the what is of something, must be experienced?

This is what the 'objectivists' believe; those people who not only assume that it is possible to share experiences but that shared experiences are what compose reality. But objectivity, like the idea of sharing, is presumed not ascertained. The only certainty is the experience of the individual who *I* am, here and now, and alone. By contrast, the assumed sharing of experience is rare in the gentle poverty of the splendid void where we cannot see others. But poverty is the nucleus of all wealth, as the void is the vacuum drawing in all existence. In the world, the shared experience is an attempt to define, to prolong, to control, to own, to manipulate, to supplant. In the splendid void, however, we grapple with our impotency in a minimalist, yet audience-safe environment, whose dramaturgical arc is designed to heighten the experience of choice-in-the-moment.

The audience response, however, is not a conditioned knowledge or expectation, but rather a stimulation of the elements interacted with in the space. If we struggle within the void, then it is because we have forgotten how to break down the cemented experiences we have accumulated over a lifetime within culture and that in our minds have become universals. We forget that our experiences remain subjective and, at most, intersubjective with the experiences of others, when in culture they are expressed by language. For those who navigate Hentschläger's splendid void without difficulty, choice becomes consciousness pronounced, as much as do sensation and experience – with the three composing the consciousness at hand. But before we can build on this realization, we hear someone nearby (for we cannot see through the fog) succumbing to the anxiety of the newness, the effect of the loss of perceptual boundaries on someone in the audience not ready or resilient enough to take the challenge.

Deadened reception, commonly misunderstood as 'boredom' and the opposite of panic – is another symptom that becomes pronounced by the splendid void, in participants with a low threshold of curiosity and enthrallment. For these people, the construct of a physical plenum of experience has little value. In contrast to the audience who leaves enthralled, the deadened leave feeling insufficiently stimulated. Yet for the incurious, just as for the enthralled, the elimination of walls, ceiling and objects in the Hentschläger void, effects a dramatic phenomenological reduction. Though sober, it is an ambient and minimalist-conceptualist sound-and-sightscape, not unlike the abstract painting of the first half of the 20th century or the Structuralist films of the midcentury. And it effects this reduction without directly referencing histories. For like reductionist painting or sculpture, the splendid void makes us aware of the essential structure of the experienced moment. Though we ordinarily forget that there is a floor beneath our feet, and beneath that the earth, by the

time that we emerge from the splendid void installation, the impoverishment of our senses has reawakened us to our gravitational support. We of course always assume the earth is there, but unless we are compelled to expand from a void that repeats our earliest infantile experience of emerging into a world of light, space and gravity, the memory of that infantile experience remains forever lost to us. The Hentschläger void re-enacts our first infantile experience of emerging from the womb; first in depriving us of the ordinary sensation of sight, then in our stepping out of the splendid void as we experience re-emergence into the world.

A curtain opened to the infinitude

The elaborate programming and painstaking engineering of a structure and poetics of immersive interactions with light, form, motion, color and ambience, Hentschläger calibrates along a timeline using custom audio-visual-spatial instruments, to prompt the audience's performance. What the audience experiences is neither random nor vaguely unintentional in its activation of the minds of the audience to navigate through a plenum of fog that is analogous to the infinitude. It may strike us as ironic that the obstruction of emerging fog can be likened to a curtain opened to the infinite. We cannot see, but we nonetheless extend out, feel with our hand, and inch forward to find that the obstruction is only visual. We extract from this experience – very like experiences in our infancy, before our eyes catch up with our limbs – that the *obstruction* is in fact a *sight* or indeed *insight* needed to transcend the obstruction to our minds and limbs. We learned the opposite some months or years after infancy; that a plate of glass or a mirror does not obstruct our vision though it does obstruct our limbs. This phenomenological parameter is not yet incorporated into SOL, FEED or ZEE. But it is implied, even if we do not realize it is implied, by one experience of a sense or faculty being obstructed by one material, as other senses or another sense or faculty may not be.

To truly grasp the extreme deprivation of cultural meaning of the installations, we must discipline our language by banishing all adjectives except for those that reference the physical qualities of experience, which act more truly as nouns in naming an experience than values qualifying experience, as most adjectives do. We refer to light that induces experiences of colors – black and white, red and blue, etc. – but not light that is beautiful or unsettling, even psychologically associative. A temperature may be burning, hot, temperate, cold, or freezing, but not comfortable or debilitating. These refer again to experiences as values, and are a step up from the ultimate reduction desired, however restrained they remain. The aim of the splendid void is to detach from the cultural values that frame the singular experience of the individual in the instant, with an unwanted collective and consensual history that heaps collective relations onto the individual reduction.

Lights lower – blackness – fog seeps through the space – I move slowly – feel the floor – extend hands – collision – another body – who? – recoil sideways – ahead – ohh – a wall – step right – another step – another – begin to see – gray – white – yellowish – begin to feel – moist – warm air thickens – sudden wind – flash – blindness – blackness there – grayness emerges – turns white – afterimage – spherical light – black corona – intercepted cool air current blows in – turns warm in stasis – temples throbbing – breathing regular, irregular, regular again – heartbeat – pulse – pulse – PULSE – !PULSE! – stop listening – stop feeling – breathe – can't – breathe – can't – breathe – can – can – breathe – light – bodies – too many – move left – more left – can breathe – normal – breath – is – normal – stroboscope – pulse lights – illuminate fog – feel it – softened and evenly dispersed – creating kaleidoscopic hues – two – three – fog thickens – forming – forms – no – yes! – forms a screen – for light – focus – taking form as – image – object – structure – human? – no – animation – humanoid – fog density

accumulating – humidity – anxiety rising – yellow hue – floor underfoot – steadiness temples throbbing – breathing regular, irregular, regular again – heartbeat – pulse – pulse – PULSE – !PULSE! – stop – breathe – can't – breathe – can't – breathe – can – can – breathe – light – bodies – can breathe – normal – breath – is – normal – stroboscope – pulse lights – illuminate fog – feel it – softened and evenly dispersed – creating kaleidoscopic hues – two – three – four-dimensional structures in constant animation – Nothing solid. Wall? Where is the wall? Feel with feet. The floor! I still have the floor. And the earth. There must be the earth beneath it. Light – beam – projection – bodies – colliding – floating – mid air – somersaulting – floating in space

A loss of sensory control within a security zone

In a Hentschlägerian *immersion* into the *void*, the objects that ordinarily are the reference points of our rationalization of experience, and its history in totality as the physical world, are deferred, rendered invisible, and obstructed from view. This enables us to sort out the structure of consciousness, except that in place of reasoning we will be sensing an experience that demarcates the border of the objective and subjective structures of the body-mind. In other words, Hentschläger establishes for his participants a zone of security and stability within which we may at our own rate of time and emotion react to being deprived of identifiable objects that we associate with culture, and before it with consciousness. With the removal of object referents that define the space of shared, architectural and natural reality, we are shrouded in fog, darkness and light, color and sound; the media by which he effects our general loss of sensory control. The loss is not total enough to effect pandemonium. We feel assured that the floor will not give way beneath our feet, that blades or other forms of torture will not eviscerate us. We remain secure enough to surrender control to the sudden and momentary degrees of blindness we've consented to in exchange for a heightened attainment of nonperceptual consciousness.

The consciousness that Hentschläger's SOL, FEED and ZEE reduces, is that of infantile sensation, before we coagulate it into metaphors and objects that then become confused as truths. Another analogy is that we revert to a near-unconscious state, yet conscious enough to see colors and motion, and hear sounds; all indiscernible, and all without reference to objective experience. The difference again is we have agreed to conduct this reduction socially, that is together, with one social construct that mediates our experiences – so long as we remain within a comfort zone. In this way we can experience instances of new experience for which we have no words, and usually these are complex experiences, confusing because they are composed of multiple phenomena that we have not yet broken down. Once we begin to break the experiences down, we begin to use language by identifying the components of the experience with such concepts as *green, bright, fog, flashes, throbbing, suffocating, moist, sweet, humid, warm, pungent* and then grow physiologically and psychologically complex with identifications such as *delight, disorientation, imbalance, anxiety, confusion, panic, overwhelmed.*

Yet on an unconscious level, we have retained the construct and medium of language to keep us in contact with culture. This is obvious as we read this attempt at reduction, in which we see words that compel us to think of experiences. We are not conscious of words amid the fog and flashes of ZEE, but we are conscious that we can identify what we experience – otherwise we would panic. Some do panic, and when they do, it is because they have lost all ties with not only their conscious language, but with culture and even memory; at least the memory of being within a safely controlled environment.

It is afterwards, when we return from our reduction to simple experience of the senses without concerning ourselves with

communication of it, that we become aware that language must now mediate the experience or else it will be lost to our ability to rationalize it. But before we call this mediation an intrusion on the experience, we must consider that language has mediated our every experience since we emerged from our infantile self-absorption. What we can be certain of is that when we return from the Hentschläger immersion, we are ready to recognize that we have returned to the identification of things established by the society we inherit them from. In this case we return to art and science, which is a translation of experience into models of objective truth and the technology that objectivity makes possible. In place of objectivity, the splendid void can, with considerable reflection, make us more aware that despite all of the cultural constructs we believe to share, the Hentschlägerian reduction brings us closer to understanding that we do not really know that they are shared. We only know that we say they are.

The philosophy of experience

What is the value of the subjective experience we have emerged from? What is the value of what can be shared from the experience? (Which is really only the language used to convey the experience, not the experience itself.) And what consensus or lack thereof can be arrived at in comparing language accounts of the reduction? Only participants in a Hentschläger void can answer such questions. And yet, in the context of what for well over a century theorists have called phenomenology – or the philosophy of experience – Hentschläger achieves with elegance and brevity, with our permission upon entering one of his voids, what the phenomenologists have labored over with mixed results, in their attempts to conduct readers or listeners to core existence through their own reduction of experience. But of course readers and listeners will be frustrated when using only the media of language to conduct their ideological reconstructions of something that cannot truly be reconstructed – especially not with words. With the luxury of experiential deprivation, Hentschläger avoids words, spatially limiting the audience's sense experience of space-time arrangements, so as to hone the events of our consciousness, cognition, perception and sensation for a prearranged time and space.

How could Hentschläger not improve upon the philosophers in replacing the lecture with an engineered interactive installational modulation of space, fog, strobes; ambient surround sound and colored light; moisture, temperature, and other physical inducements to our perception and sensations? It is pure experience, not logic or words, that enables an audience largely untrained, yet moderately prepared, to experiment and leave behind their arsenals of intuition, rhetoric and scholarship, suspending belief in a world-reality, so as to reduce to a state of awareness conducive to experiencing isolated sensations of phenomena and the psychological states that respond to and define them for us.

For the more questioning participants, Hentschläger provides opportunities to interact; for his audiences to experience, if not through which to understand, that our consciousness is not merely a *knowing* that occurs *in the mind* in isolation from the world, but an awareness of the self interacting with things other than and beyond the control of the self. *Stop! Breathing. Stop! Breathing. Stop! Breathing.*

If Hentschläger compels his audiences to reduce their experiences of a defined moment in time and space to the bare minimum of life-sustaining structures, he also affects an experience similar to a primordial or infantile sensation. Usually it is a vague, yet physical and temporal, perception of ambiance itself through the use of fog, light, darkness, air flow, gravitational support and modulation of events; air currents, flashes of light, blackouts, obstacles to movement, comfort and discomfort zones – facilitating our attempts to experience the most we

can – *!Flash! – afterimage – sphere of light – center black – center blue – center purple – spots off to parameter – trails up – trails down, sliding left, snaking south – music – in my head – no, far off.* Hentschläger seems to shut off all but the basic components of physical and perceptual events. In phenomenological terms he is really isolating them for us to rediscover and re-experience them as discreet and discontinuous phenomena outside our control. And it is only through becoming comfortable with our lack of control that we expand our capacity to intake the infinite.

This heightened experience of the physical world, even for the less inquisitive, comes as a rediscovery of our first infantile experiences of sensations that under his mediation are encountered as enhanced, even emboldened consciousness, of our relation to thingness in the world. The renewed consciousness is the result of Hentschläger's isolation of objects and events from the culture and language that we normalize everyday by – *surround – suction – reflection – recognition – reck – cognition – reck – collection – reck – creation – reck – conciliation* – into more familiar and integrated contexts (home, school, work, exteriors) and under more psychologically complex conditions (entertainment, study, exertion, arousal). One such complexity is the obstruction of the space that is in front, behind, to the sides, and all around us up to our noses. Fog is the obstruction; *fog* is the infinite.

A phenomenological reduction

Attempts by mystics to self-induce transcendence can be compared to the minute and sober epiphanies that may arise out of Hentschläger's installational immersions. They are also akin to the experiments of scientists and positivist philosophers to identify an unassailably formal and objective reality only through logic and models of unbiased verification. In other words, Hentschläger delivers us to the cliff overlooking the splendid void without pushing us into its abyss.

The difference is, whereas the mystics and the positivists failed to confirm for others that mysticism or positivism can transcend culture, Hentschläger – like the Chinese and Japanese Zen artists, and the Indian Tantric artists of bygone centuries, and painters such as Kandinsky, Malevich, Klee and Mondrian in the 20th century – affords us the formulas to reduce from the world so as to experience the components that make up that world. Of course, ultimately, we cannot void ourselves of culture or even subjective mediation to experience a truly, pure sensation – whatever 'truly' and 'pure' may mean. But we can reduce our consciousness of its basic constituents of perception of mediated color and light; form and mass; temperature, and other consciousness of sensations within the world.

I will not here burden our attempt to reduce to a state of perception that precedes enculturation, by recalling prior attempts of such 20th century phenomenologists as Husserl, Heidegger, Merleau-Ponty, Levinas, Sartre or Farber to distinguish consciousness from cognition and cognition from culture; which means to separate to the subjective (first person, unshared, unrepeatable) experience from objective (third person, shared, repeatable upon demand) knowledge. I will only suggest that Hentschläger confirms the conviction that we can exercise a *phenomenological reduction*. And this enables us to experience, isolate, identify and rationalize perceptions that are ordinarily experienced as a part of culture and or nature, as if we had returned to an infantile state of entry into a world outside of our control, but now armed with the experience, lessons and memory of having grown through that culture and nature. Yet how can this be?

Though it is questionable to what degree the immersive reduction of Hentschläger has divorced the participants from sharable cultural and natural experience, to the extent that the individual experience of each participant can be said to be the only subjective and unsharable sensation, perception and cognition of the experience;

upon returning to the experience of the immersion and reduction through the memory of it afterwards, the essential experience can be defined without doubt in cultural terms, as the isolation of the self from the other selves we cannot see.

Upon the diminished capacity of vision to either periods of darkness or near total fog, we can either relish or be disturbed by the realization that our diminished vision will be reducing us to a state which heightens our experience of hearing, touch, and to a lesser degree, smell and taste. It especially heightens our experience of the functions of our own body, such as our heart rate, flow of blood, breathing, perspiration, need to expel waste; all of which may be uncomfortable and cause anxiety in the beginning because we are so unaccustomed to such a degree of culturally unmediated experience.

Here we are then in a Hentschlägerian plenum of phenomena indulging our phenomenological body as it rarely has the luxury to be indulged. Even the anxiety we feel at the outset is a luxury, in that we can feel secure knowing that our safety has been secured, so that even our anxiety can be experienced as a revelation to feel. Given all that has been stated here, let us all now reduce to a state of sensation and perception without words.

The end of the term *phenomenology*

In expanding out of our Hentschlägerian phenomenology back to culture, back to nature, we have no reason not to enjoy the vanity that we have all just experienced the phenomenological reduction that philosophers have been debating for millennia. Congratulations. The term *phenomenology* need never again be defined for us, as we have experienced it now ourselves.

Now we are ready to experience the growth of phenomenology into mythopoetics. Were we of a mythopoetical mind at the time of our immersion into reductionist fog, we would not end with the descriptive phase of abstract sense-data. We would expand that sense data – say the sensation of fog – beyond phenomenology into the modality of myth. We may at once summon to mind the creation myths of the world, which are nothing if not analogs of the primitive or infantile experience of discovering the world of otherness as it emerges from the informe – in this case Hentschläger's fog – that is, from the vague and undefined contours and differentiations in tone, light and shadow that appear amid the fog and that the mythopoetic faculty of the mind extends into oceans of formlessness. And that informe appears again in the late stages of senile deliquescence of meaningful form – the gradual breakdown of hard edges and distinct surfaces into nebulous fields that fade into the shadow of the unconsciousness of dementia adumbrating the demise of perception, intelligence, and finally the approach of death.

We can, by the mythopoetic experience, pass through to all the inferential leaps of the mystic. Now we are ready for FEED and it's hyperemulation of Blake's souls; except that in Hentschläger's work they are soulless drones without control over the algorithms that determinate the direction, speed, and congregational patterns in simulated bodies and clouds. We here are still effecting a reduction in not allowing ourselves to extrapolate meanings from the experience beyond those of the moment. We do not participate in recalling some Vedic or Egyptian creation myth elicited by the enveloping fog. Instead we remain true to our reductions, an indifference that isolates us from the mystic and the poet. But in tow with this reduction we can now consider Kurt Hentschläger's ZEE and SOL as phenomenological reductions to genuine and irreducible and unmediated sensation that is the end of the phenomenological impetus sought by philosophers.

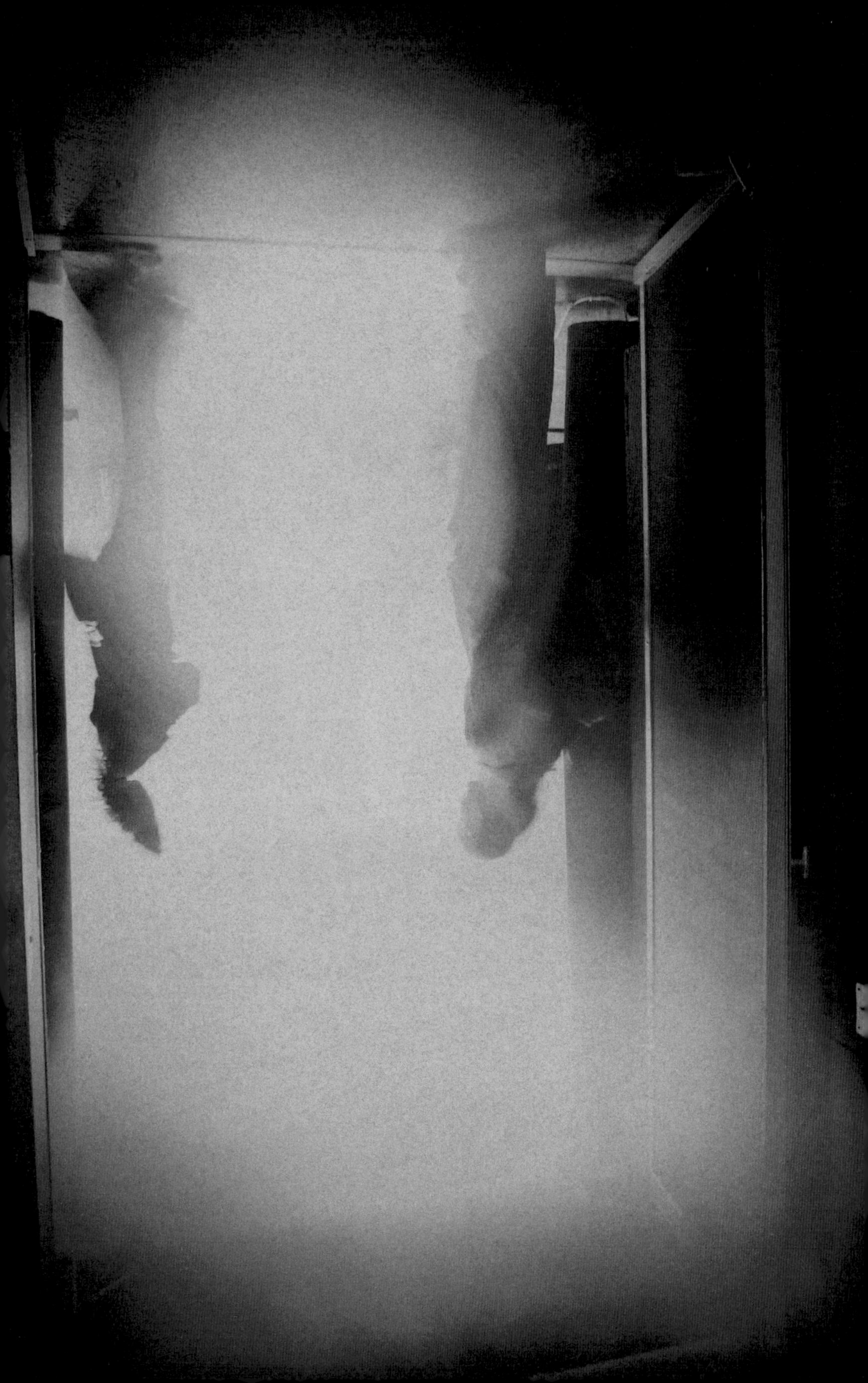

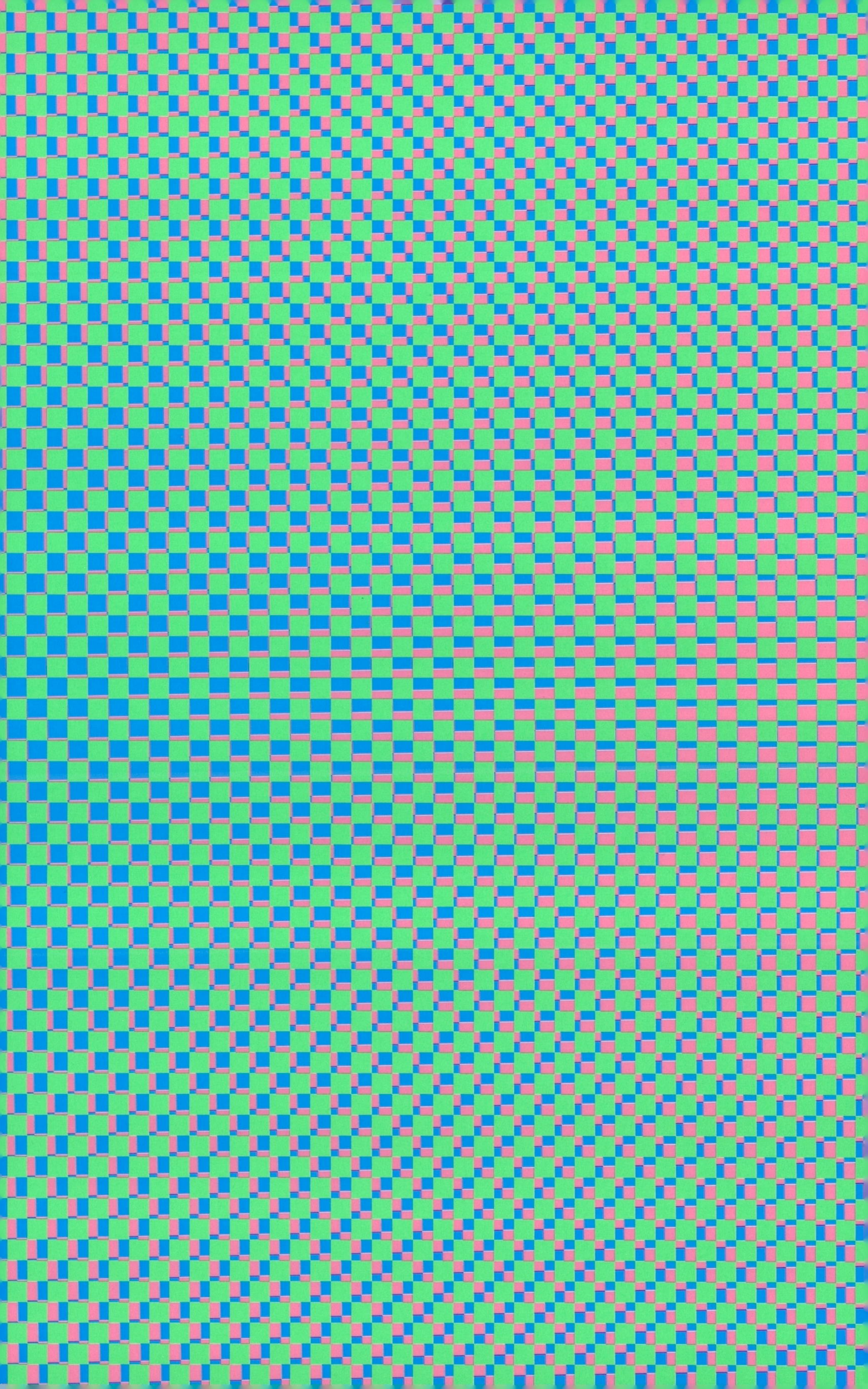

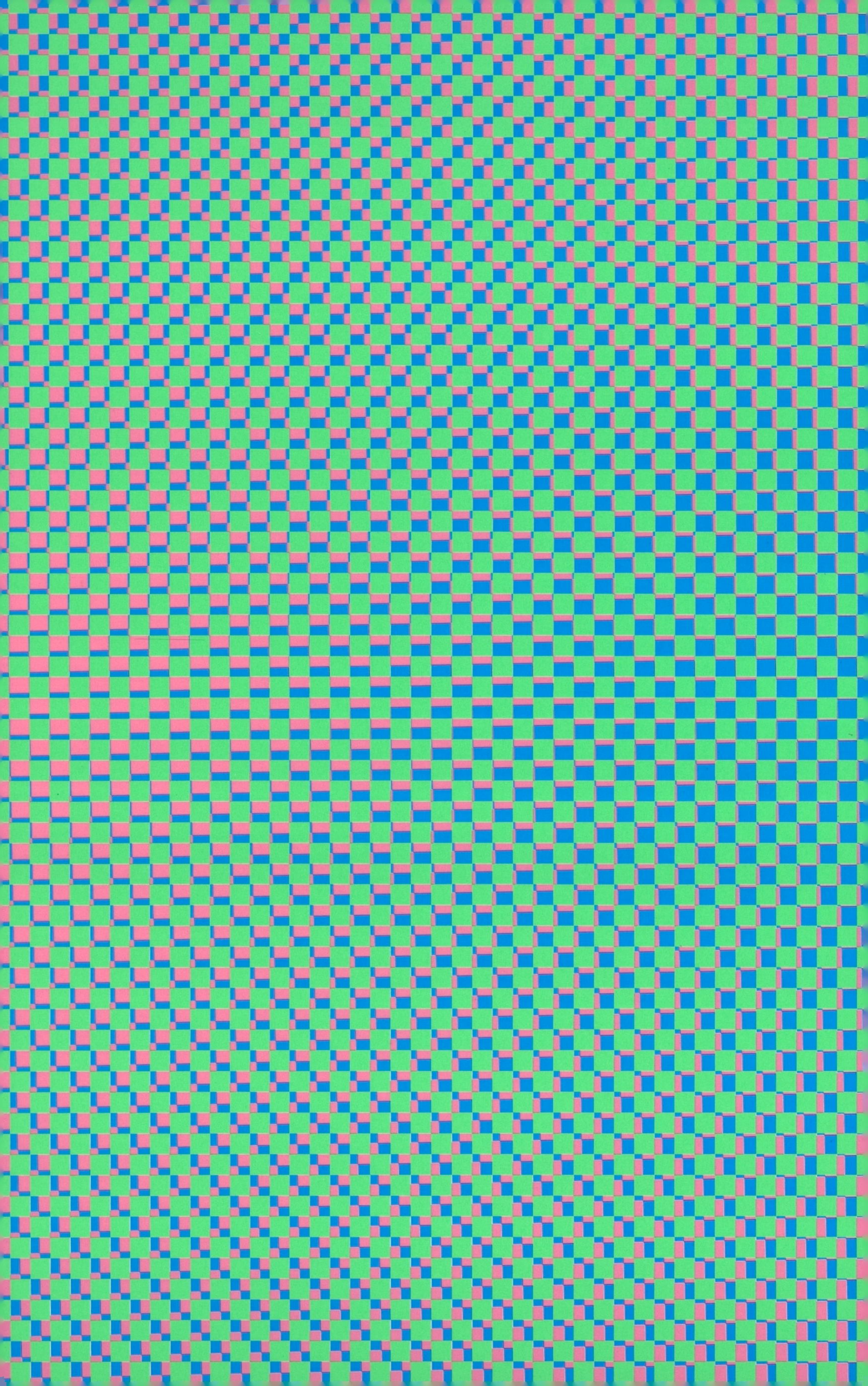

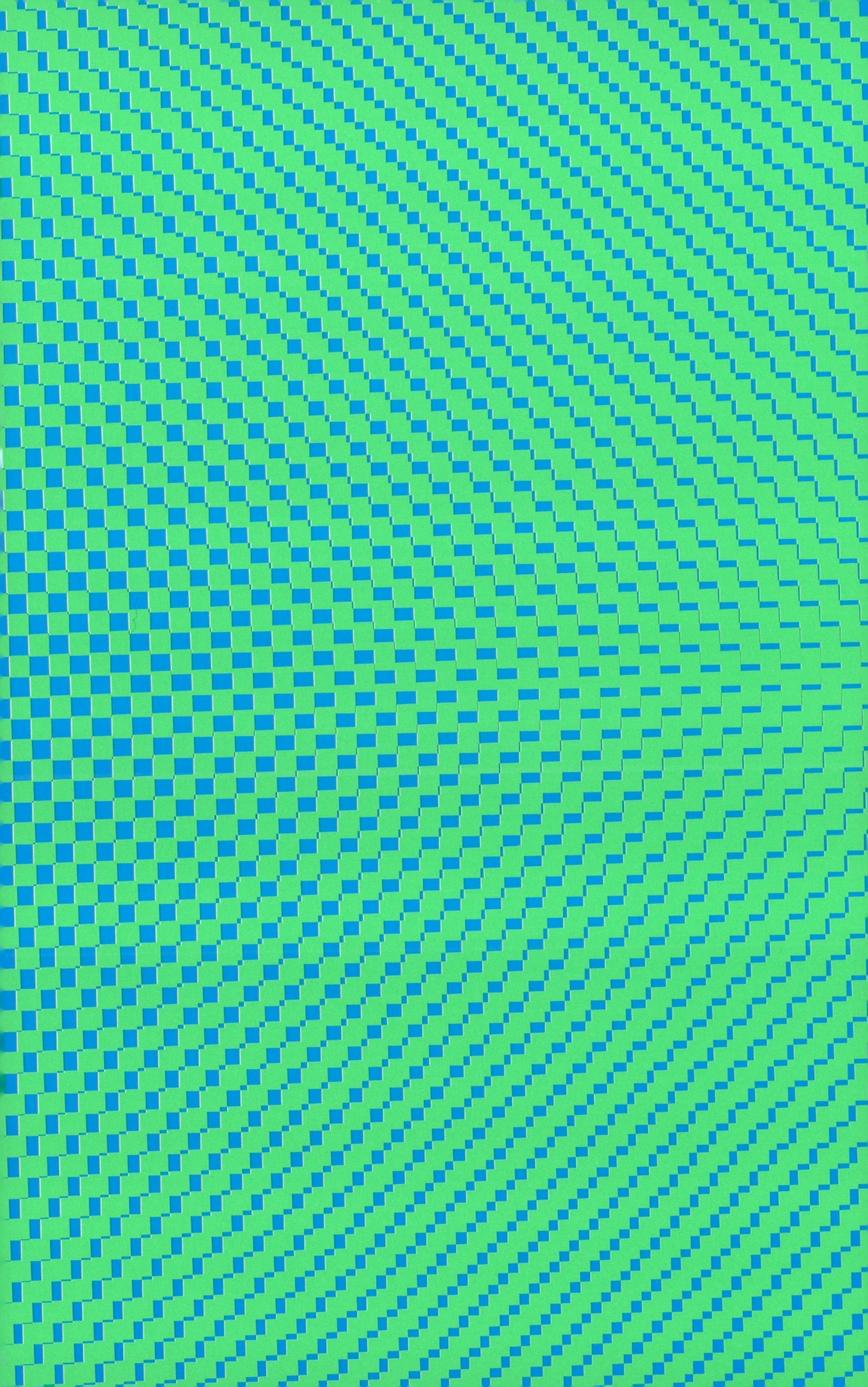

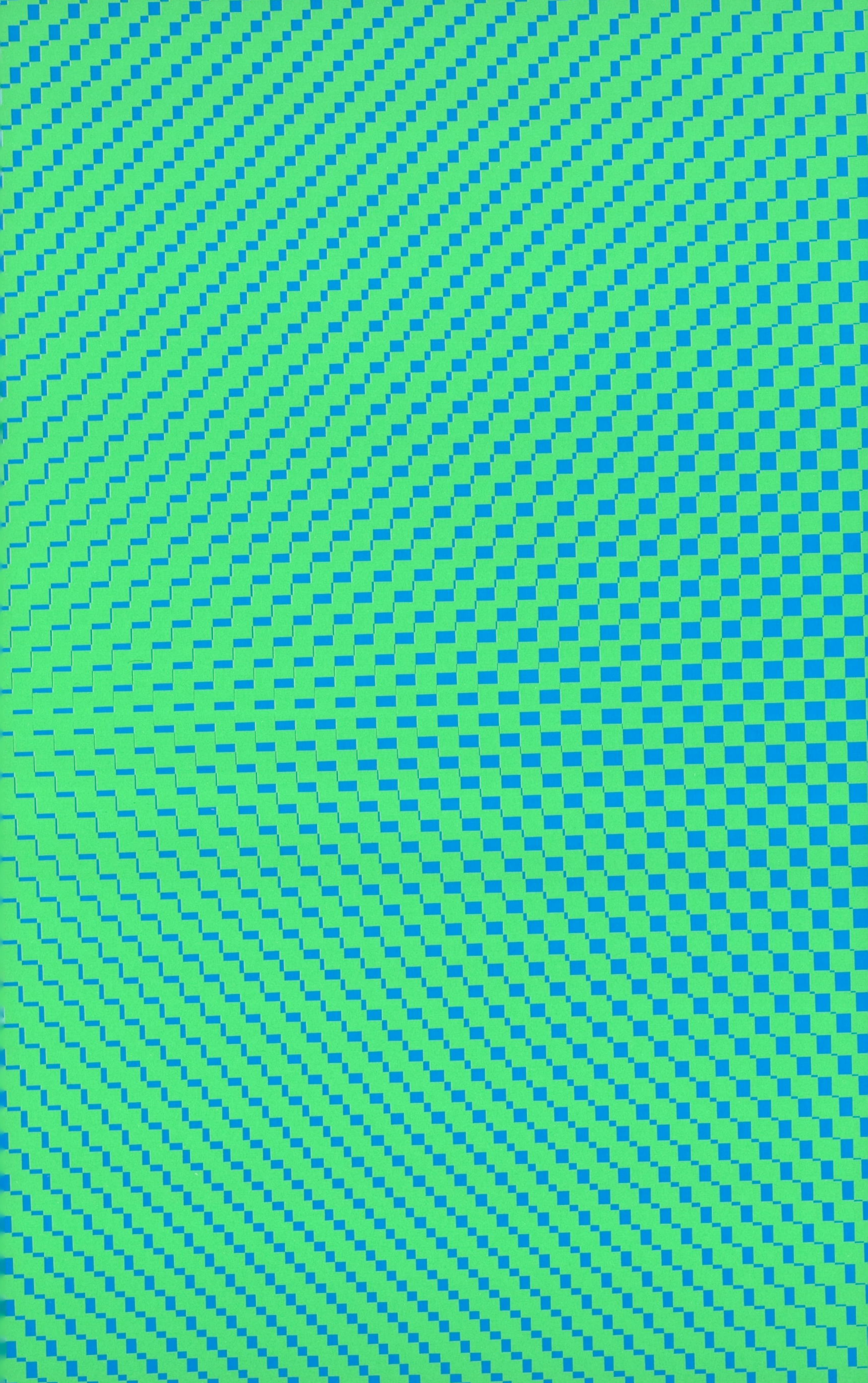

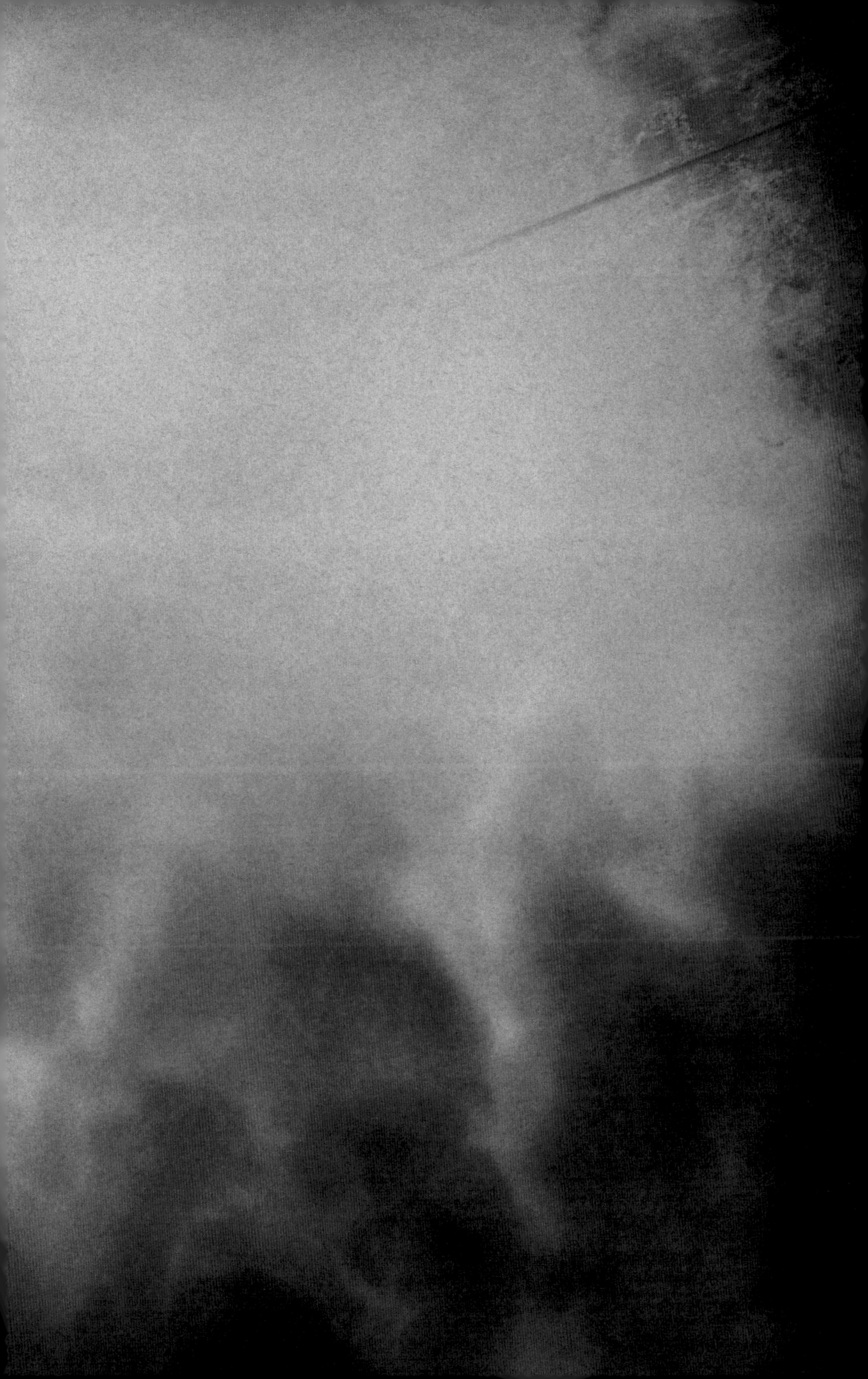

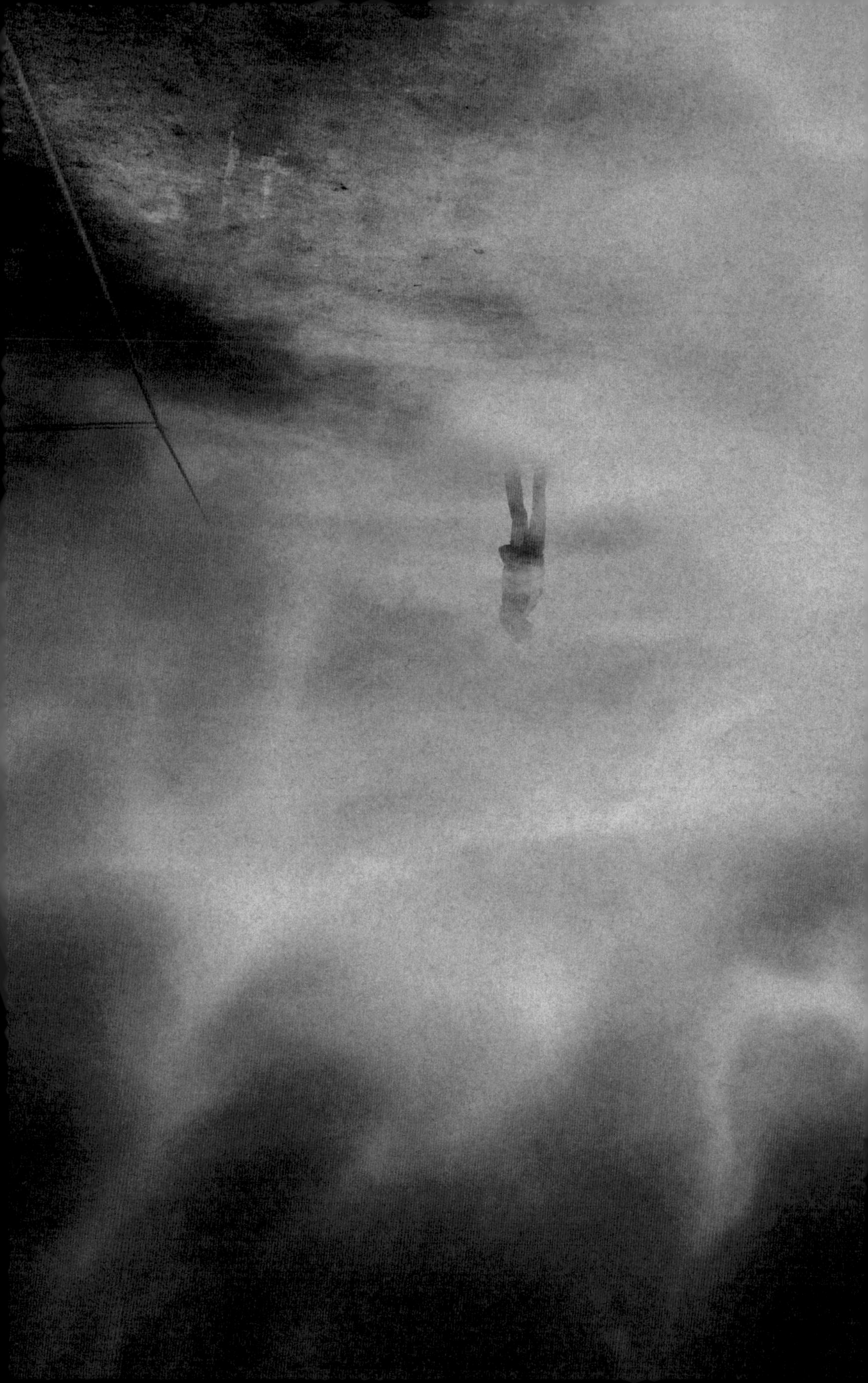

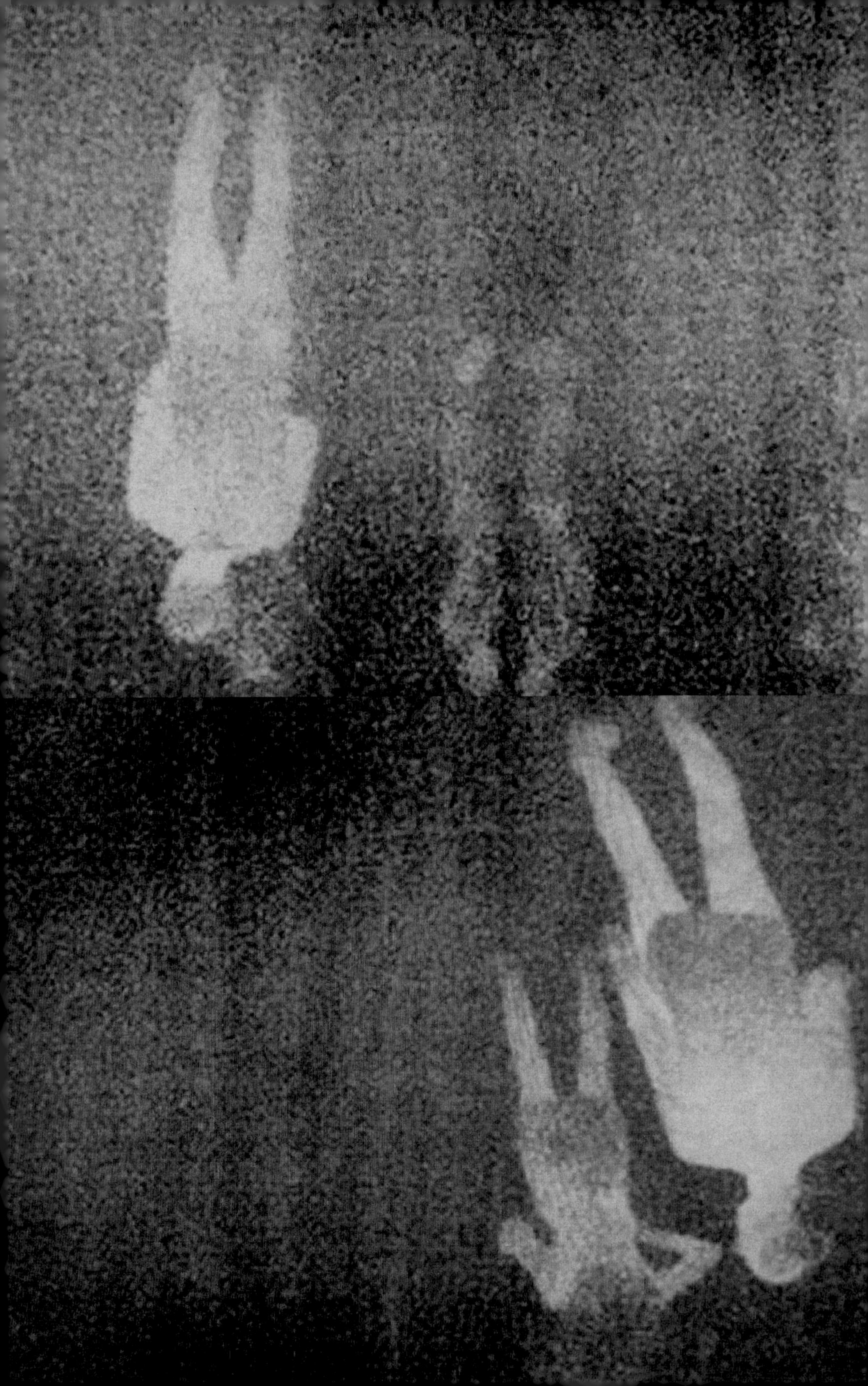

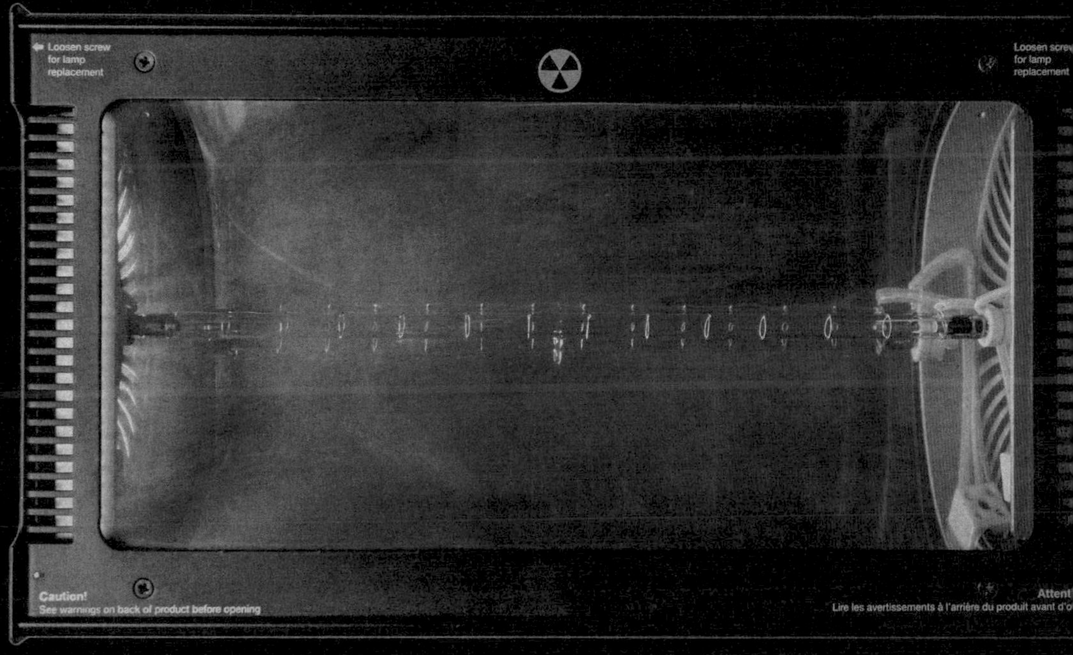
Loosen screw
for lamp
replacement
for lamp
replacement
Caution!
See warnings on back of product before opening
Lire les avertissements à l'arrière du produit avant

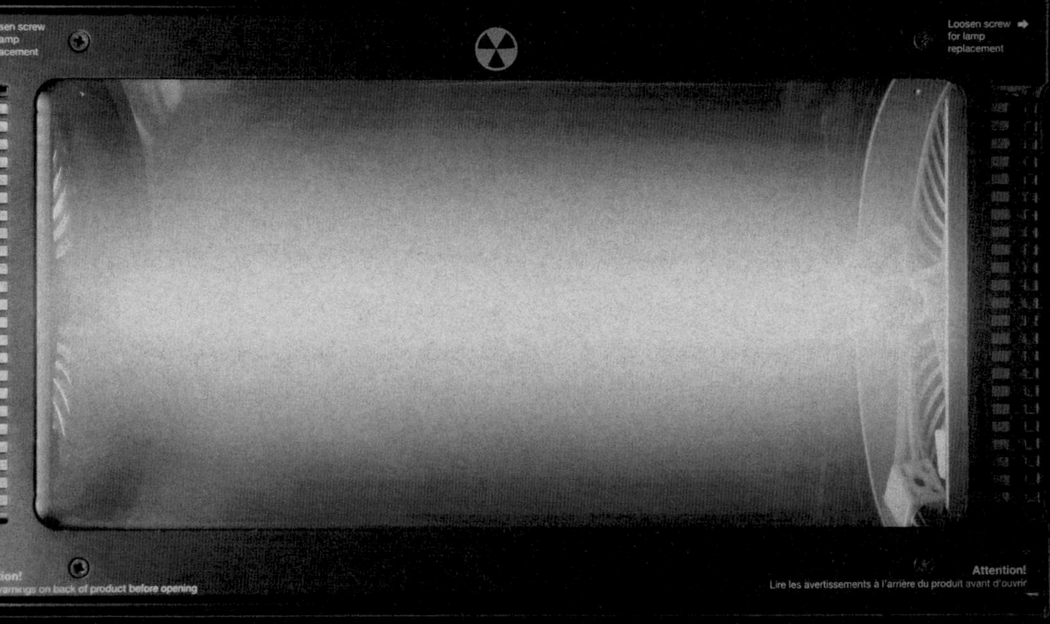
Loosen screw for lamp replacement
Loosen screw for lamp replacement
warnings on back of product before opening
Attention!
Lire les avertissements à l'arrière du produit avant

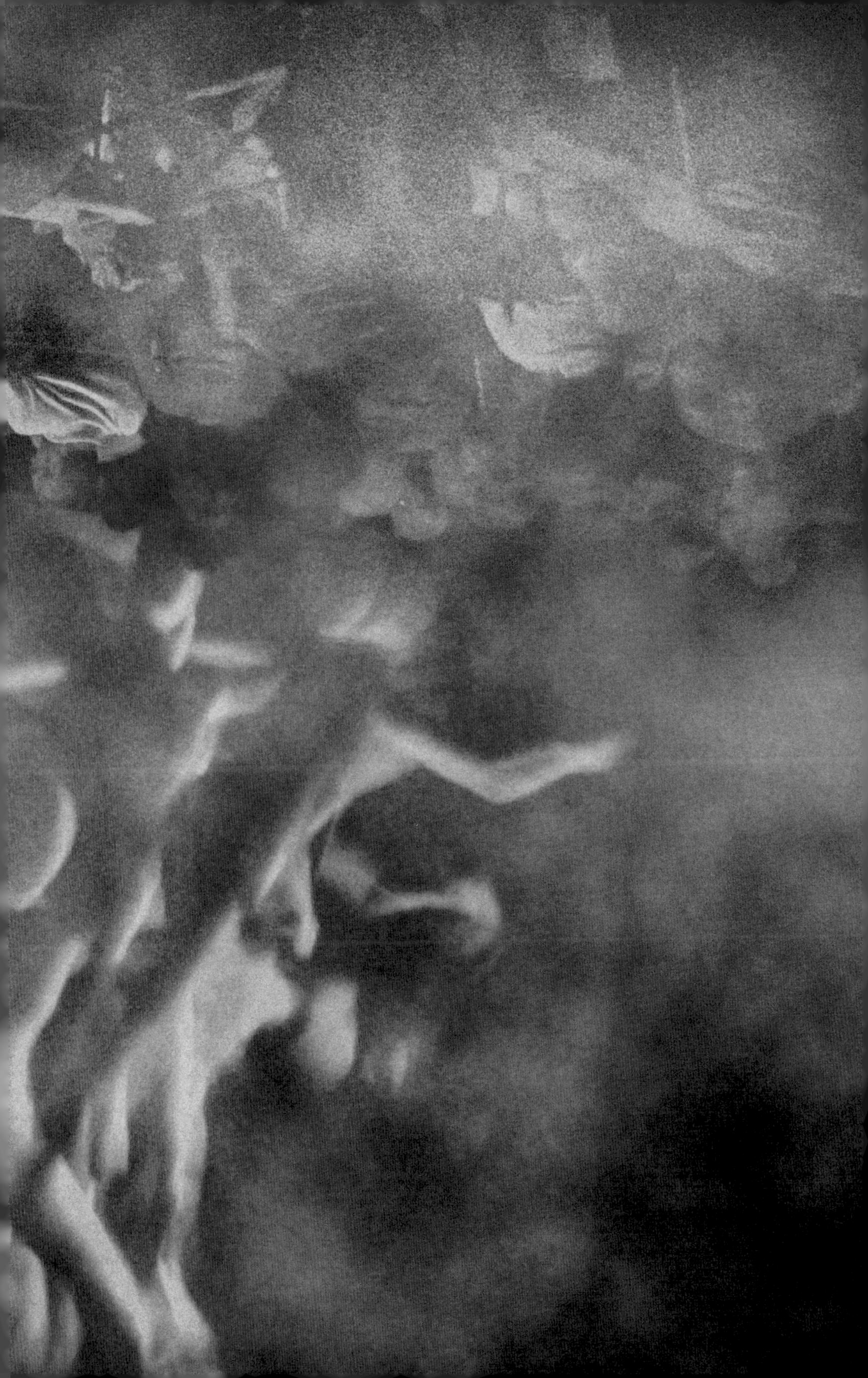

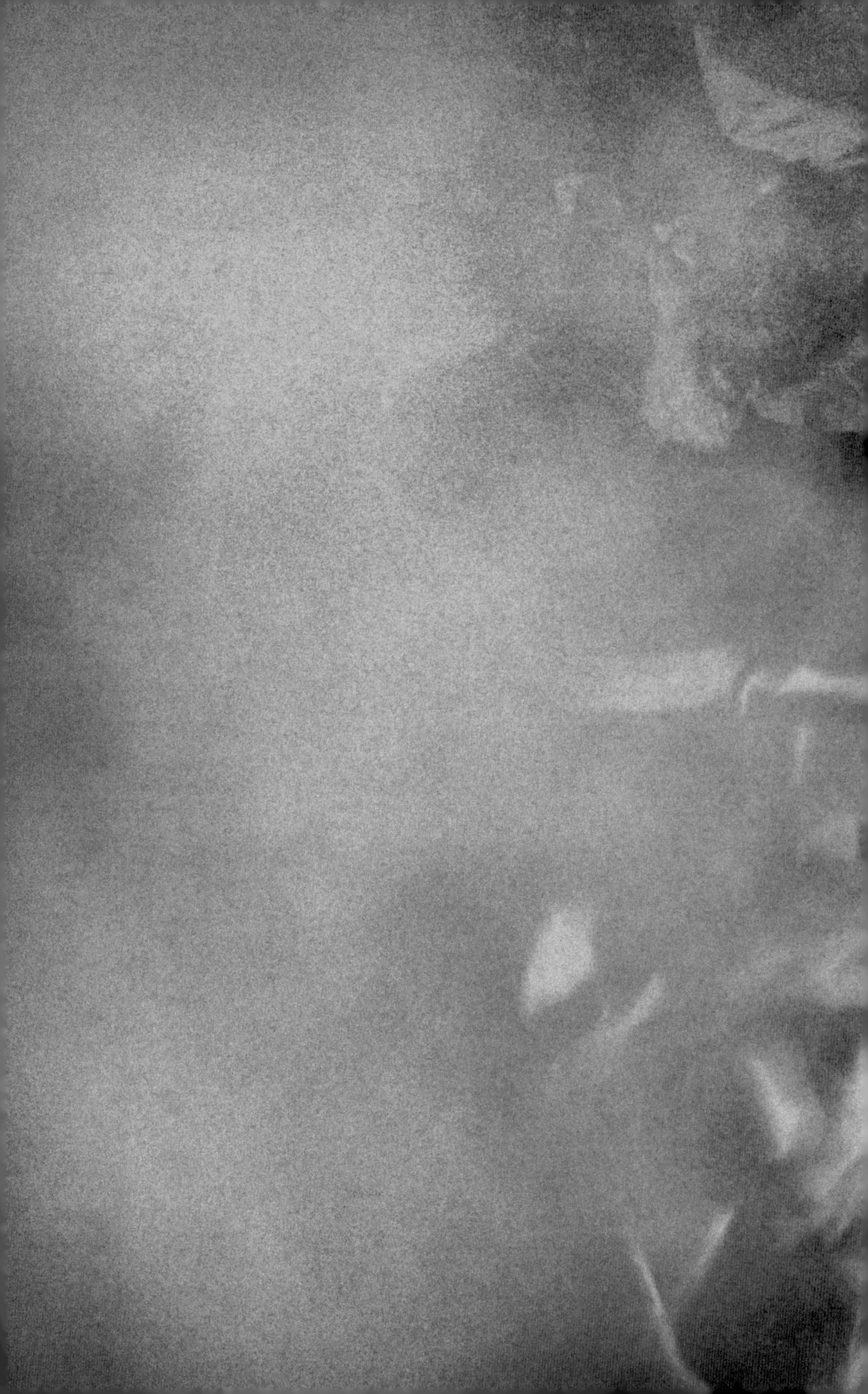

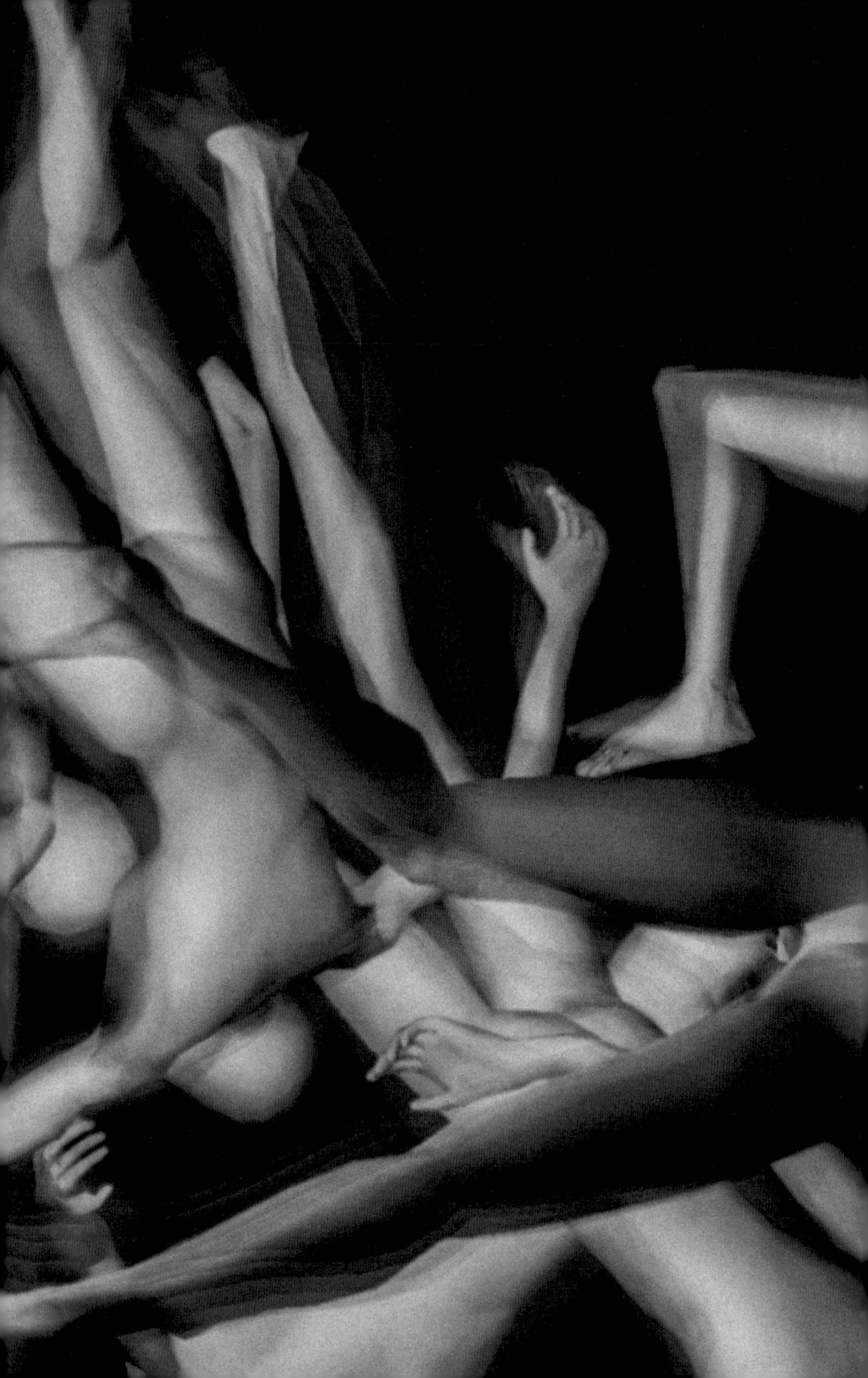

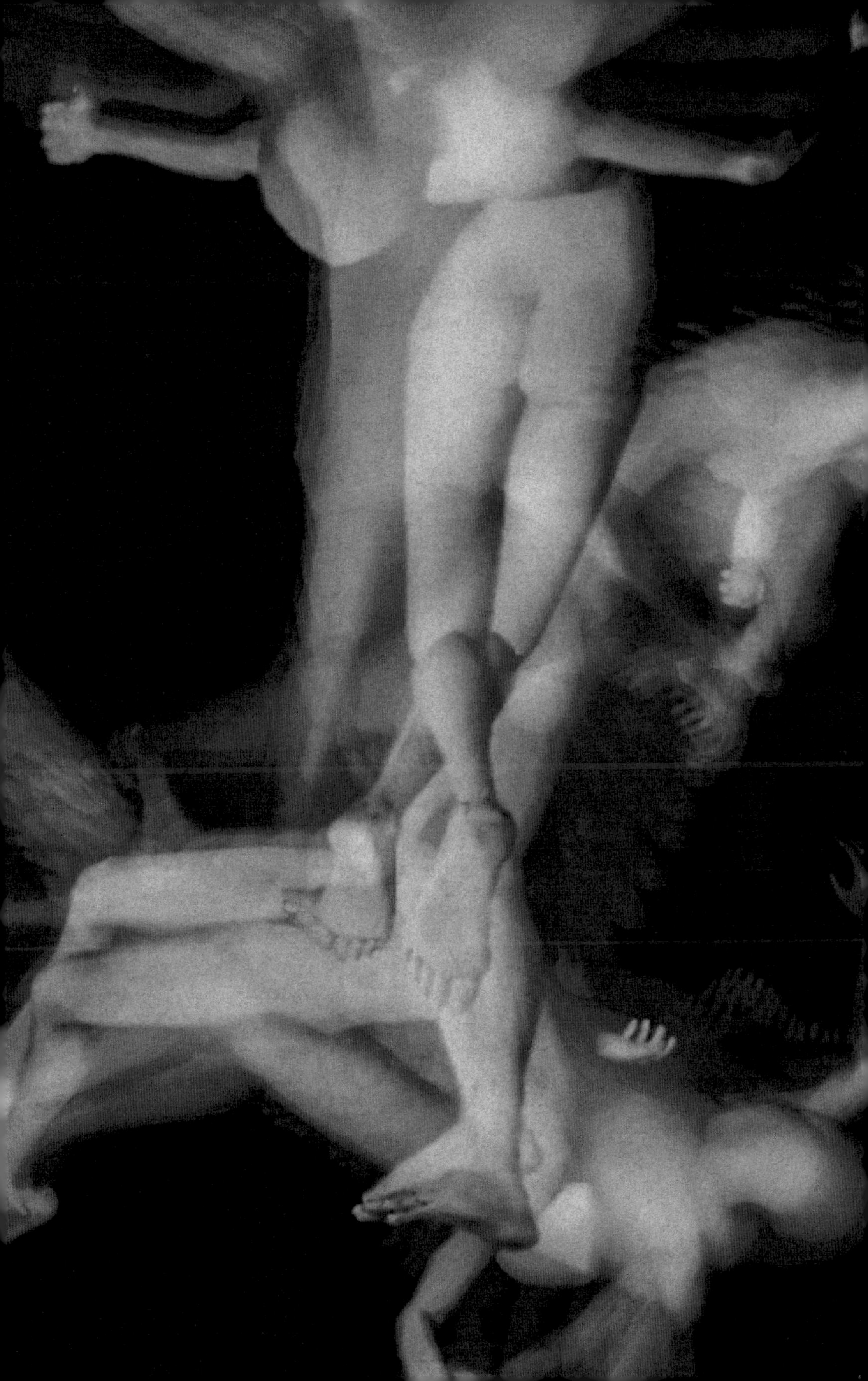

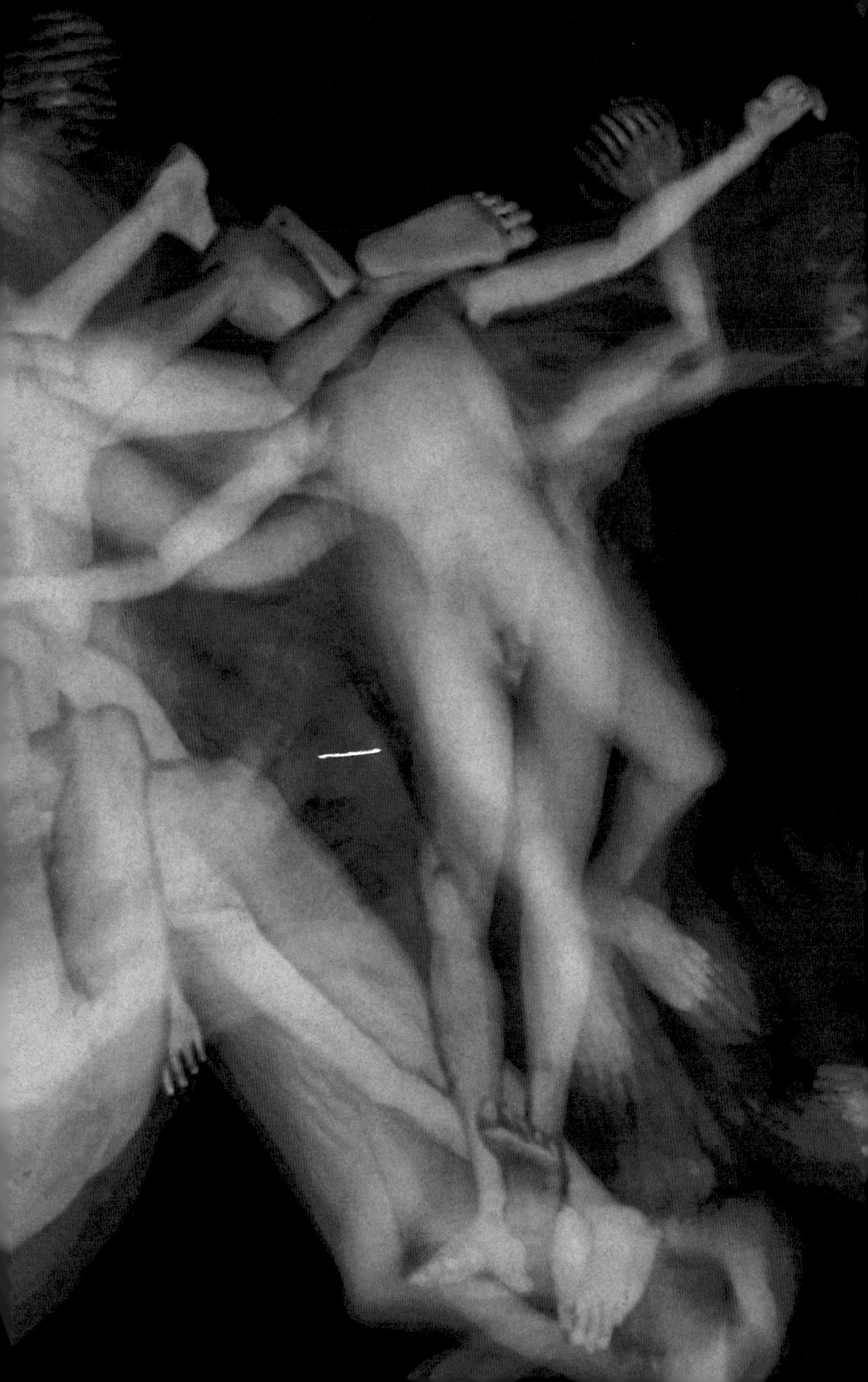

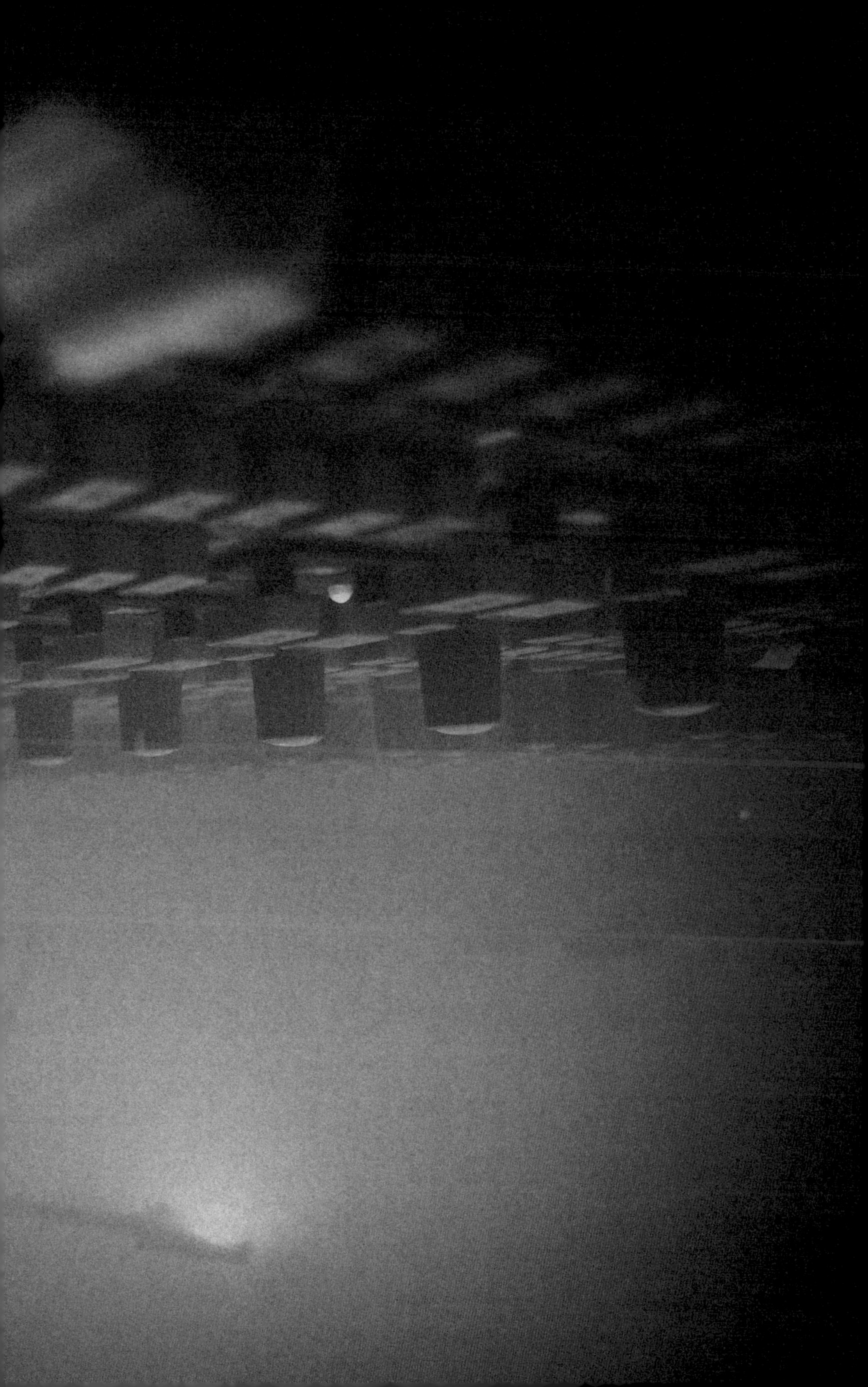

Kurt Hentschläger

Born in Linz, Austria and currently based in Chicago, Kurt Hentschläger creates immersive audiovisual installations and performances. Between 1992 and 2003 he worked collaboratively within the artist duo *Granular-Synthesis.*

Selected presentations of his work include: the Biennale Arte, Venice and the Biennale Teatro, Venice; the Stedelijk Museum, Amsterdam; MoMA PS1, New York; MAC Musée d'art contemporain de Montréal; MAK Museum of Applied Arts, Vienna; ZKM Center for Art and Media, Karlsruhe; the National Art Museum of China, Beijing; the National Museum for Contemporary Art, Seoul; ICC InterCommunication Center, Tokyo; the Laboratorio Arte Alameda, Mexico City; Mona Museum of Old and New Art, Hobart, Tasmania; the Sharjah Art Foundation, Sharjah.

Currently, Hentschläger is a Visiting Artist at SAIC, the School of the Art Institute of Chicago.

kurthentschlager.com

Thanks to:
Martin Sturm, Genoveva Rückert, Richard Castelli, Florence Berthaud, Claire Dugot, Chara Skiadelli, G. Roger Denson, Isabelle Meiffert, Detlev Pusch, Alexander Böhmler, Pablo Monterrubio-Benet, Yan Zhou, Ursula Hentschläger, Claudia Hart, Peter Paul Kainrath, CTM

Artist Representation:
Richard Castelli / Epidemic

Exhibitions of SOL, ZEE, FEED

OL

Co-commissioned by the OK Center for Contemporary Art, Linz, Austria
Co-produced by CTM – Festival for Adventurous Music and Art, Berlin, Germany

2017 OK Center for Contemporary Art, Linz, Austria
2017 *Fear Anger Love*, CTM – Festival for Adventurous Music and Art, Berlin, Germany

EE

Co-commissioned by the OK Center for Contemporary Art, Linz, Austria and Wood Street Galleries, Pittsburgh, PA, USA

2016 Romaeuropa Festival, MACRO Museum of Contemporary Art (La Pelanda), Rome, Italy
2013 *I look to you and I see nothing*, Sharjah Art Foundation, Sharjah, United Arab Emirates
Beam in Thine Own Eye, Mona Museum of New and Old Art, Hobart, Tasmania, Australia
Nemo Festival, Le Centquatre, Paris, France
Wood Street Galleries, Pittsburgh, PA, USA
2011 *Matter-Light*, Béthune, France
Abandon Normal Devices, FACT Foundation for Art and Creative Technology, Liverpool, England
2010 *dynamic (in)position*, Laboratorio Arte Alameda, Mexico City, Mexico
File Festival, São Paulo, Brazil
Wave Exhibition, INDAF Incheon International Digital Art Festival, Seoul, South Korea
2009 FuturePerfect, New York, NY, USA
STRP Festival, Eindhoven, The Netherlands
2008 Wood Street Galleries, Pittsburgh, PA, USA
Tiefenrausch, OK Center for Contemporary Art, Linz, Austria

FEED

Commissioned by the Biennale Teatro, Venice, Italy

2013 Malta Festival, Poznań, Poland
Göteborgs Dans & Teater Festival, Gothenborg, Sweden
2011 Elektra International Digital Arts Festival, Montréal, Canada
2009 Festival de Otoño, Madrid, Spain
Today's Art, Den Haag, The Netherlands
Transart, Bolzano, Italy
Figuren Theater Festival, Erlangen, Germany
Elektra International Digital Arts Festival, Montréal, Canada
2008 Elektra International Digital Arts Festival, Montréal, Canada
International Festival of Live Art, Glasgow, Scotland
Le Mois Multi 9, Quebec City, Canada
2007 STRP, Eindhoven, The Netherlands
Happy New Ears | Kunstencentrum BUDA, Kortrijk, Belgium
Ars Electronica, Linz, Austria
Sonar, Barcelona, Spain
Elektra International Digital Arts Festival, Montréal, Canada
2006 EMPAC Experimental Media and Performing Arts Center, Rensselaer Polytechnic Institute Troy, NY, USA
Impakt Festival, Utrecht, The Netherlands
Exit Festival, Paris, France
Via Festival, Mauberge, France
Netmage 06 Festival, Bologna, Italy
2005 The Biennale Teatro, Venice, Italy

Imprint

Editor
Isabelle Meiffert

Art Direction
Detlev Pusch

Texts
G. Roger Denson (4–5, 20–26)
Isabelle Meiffert (1)

Copy Editing
May Koot

Photo Credits
Kurt Hentschläger, except:
Otto Saxinger (50–51)
Detlev Pusch (53)

Color Pages
Kurt Hentschläger, Isabelle Meiffert
and Detlev Pusch (9–16, 33–48, 65–72)

Image Editing
max color, Berlin

Production Management
DISTANZ Verlag, Sonja Bahr

Production
optimal media GmbH, Röbel / Müritz

Distribution
Gestalten Berlin
www.gestalten.com
sales@gestalten.com

ISBN 978-3-95476-183-8
Printed in Germany

Published by
DISTANZ Verlag
www.distanz.de

SPLENDID VOIDS
The Immersive Works of
Kurt Hentschläger

This book has been published to
accompany the presentation of SOL:

CTM Festival for Adventurous Music and
Art, Halle am Berghain, Berlin, Germany;
January 28–February 19, 2017

OK Center for Contemporary Art, Linz,
Austria; October 21, 2017–February 25, 2018

Publication supported by

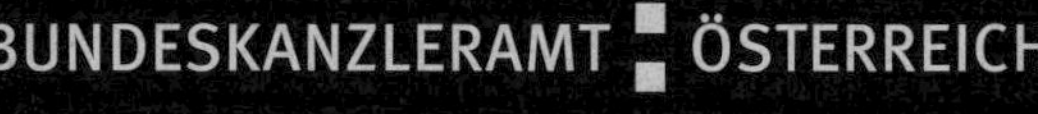

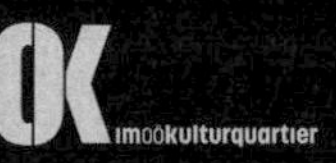

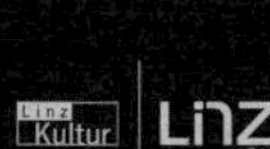